OPENBOUND

THE HUGH MacLENNAN POETRY SERIES
Editors: Allan Hepburn and Carolyn Smart

openbound

Poems of Relation

JEFFERY DONALDSON

McGill-Queen's University Press
Montreal & Kingston

ISBN 978-0-2280-2931-1 (paper)
ISBN 978-0-2280-2932-8 (ePDF)
ISBN 978-0-2280-2933-5 (ePUB)

Legal deposit fourth quarter 2026
Bibliothèque et Archives nationales du Québec

Printed in Canada on acid-free paper that is 100% ancient-forest-free, containing 100% sustainable, recycled fibre, and processed chlorine-free.

Funded by the Government of Canada | Financé par le gouvernement du Canada | Canada | Canada Council for the Arts | Conseil des arts du Canada

We acknowledge the support of the Canada Council for the Arts.

Nous remercions le Conseil des arts du Canada de son soutien.

McGill-Queen's University Press in Montreal is on land which long served as a site of meeting and exchange amongst Indigenous Peoples, including the Haudenosaunee and Anishinabeg nations. In Kingston it is situated on the territory of the Haudenosaunee and Anishinaabek. We acknowledge and thank the diverse Indigenous Peoples whose footsteps have marked these territories on which peoples of the world now gather.

Library and Archives Canada Cataloguing in Publication

Title: openbound: poems of relation / Jeffery Donaldson.

Names: Donaldson, Jeffery, 1960- author.

Series: Hugh MacLennan poetry series.

Description: Series statement: The Hugh MacLennan poetry series

Identifiers: Canadiana (print) 20260212830 | Canadiana (ebook) 20260212849 | ISBN 9780228029311 (paper) | ISBN 9780228029335 (ePUB) | ISBN 9780228029328 (ePDF)

Subjects: LCGFT: Poetry.

Classification: LCC PS8557.O527 O64 2026 | DDC C811/.54—dc23

This book was designed and typeset by Marquis Interscript in 9.5/13 Sabon.

McGill-Queen's University Press
Suite 1720, 1010 Sherbrooke St West, Montreal, QC, H3A 2R7

Authorized safety representative in the EU: Mare Nostrum Group BV, Doelen 72, 4831 GR Breda, the Netherlands, gpsr@mare-nostrum.co.uk

To us …

OPENBOUND

PROEM

Everyone had their ideas about us
and shared them freely, as though gossip
were the new new-age marriage for breeders.

Had we too been too careless, too open?
In all our searching in relationship
for the secret sauce, why keep it secret?

Privacy, if they tried to get at you,
was what they couldn't get at in public,
the part that was left out, the unsaid part.

The story makes private the story made,
in being story, as memory does,
as moments gathered do. Let's run with that.

I'll say this much. In the honestest bid
to honour ways of loving others judge,
you are the last person to be left out.

We were teacher and assistant teacher,
both ignorant. Start of term, I received
TA lists. Annette Abma. Maybe Dutch?

Unlikely characters smushed together.
With no instruction, we had neither learned
gimmicks to assist flirting with a flirt.

You would contrive to take the back-way stairs,
which left you brushing past my open door,
like a half-glimpsed and foregone conclusion.

I would feel a wind vanish from my sails
when you played truant at lecture briefings,
and then revive when, twenty minutes late,

you sauntered in, half asleep, straight from bed,
a look that asked ... if anyone might fill
this empty seat, why should it not be you?

We backed into it, the relationship.
Each of us left something to desire.
Your lack of small talk was a reticence

I bumped up against as a cold shoulder.
I was a young and not-so-easy buck
caught in the blue highlights of a Dutch Blonde,

using all my metaphors for mixing!
We were on and off for months: your patience,
my diffidence. I think of the angler

who plays out line to let the keeper run,
as long as he needs to, among the weeds.
Eventually he'll end up in a net.

Something about our early yes-and-no
seems prophetic now: what we've always been,
altogether turned, bound to be open.

We played at a form of musical chairs,
circling round the details of domicile,
skirting two- and one-bedroom flats,

waiting for the song to start. The writing
on the wall, illegible, was an ask.
If how is where, where do I want to live?

Cather's question, in *The Professor's House*,
put to my double, Professor Godfrey,
my hapless muse in all relationships.

He must let go of something, the idea
that he could only be himself (spectrum
people say this) in made-up solitude,

away from others, a cave that, clung to,
was killing him, by empty increments.
You waited patient at the opening.

One evening we sat under the great oak
in Churchill Park. Months, we'd been up and down,
then up, in tentative permanence,

which terrified as much as reassured.
Which of us spoke first? That we should promise,
since everything happens for a reason,

come what likely may, to see that we lived
interesting or disordinary lives.
Could lives be made thus up, by sole decree?

With our shared drawbacks, it was bound to be.
And what did we mean by interesting?
Armed against calamity? We called it

the Promise Tree. Time passed and the old oak
was felled. But we salvaged a rotted limb,
for interest's sake, a prosthetic promise.

How you weathered my half-assed proposal.
Thinking I'd bought a ring to say one thing,
that I dug you and thought we'd hang around,

not as rings, oh *always*, are at such times,
a true proposal. So I was the one
taken aback by what was happening.

A bent ring turning on its own compass,
I was circling nowhere in a hurry.
Poor you, an idiot for a partner,

you felt the moment mangled, naturally,
when instead I asked, "Is that what we'll do?"
hoping that you might show me what to feel.

You had the patience of long-suffering Job.
Rings now mean the world to me, metaphors
for how, in good faith, all things come about.

The fear of letting someone in my space
(for which space I mistake myself) left me
dialing 911 in last-ditch therapy!

My Freudian prescribed a four-day week
of plumbing superficial depths, the things
I'd say when someone not there also was,

in a chair behind me, just listening.
It turns out that the little back-and-forth
I feared is just what the doctor ordered.

Seemed to work. Upshot was I got our bond
reversed. People marry, then find a house.
For me the house came first, was paramount.

Attic renovations made solitude
a top point, and you gave me lots of room.
Marriage was a space to space out marriage.

Our wedding day, 17 December.
Wet snowfall the whole grayish afternoon,
slush gumming the street between home and church.

Ten to five. We stood in the house foyer,
quiet. Our time was tight. My mind racing,
I posed a question to break the silence.

Will you look after me? You said of course.
All right then. And I will look after you.
The ceremony, ceremonial,

took place at five, while our families watched.
And yet the moment we were truly bound
was in the foyer, simple Q & A.

Your warm hand in mine, as we headed out,
you used the other in the heavy slush
to hitch your white dress above galoshes.

Rilke gave us one of our wedding vows.
Each one must guard the other's solitude,
he reasons, whereby, adjoined, two loners

sich grenzen, grüssen, und schützen, that is,
border, greet, and protect one another.
It was, in ways we hardly understood,

a formula for our independence,
call it cooperative self-journeying.
Together apart, in current parlance.

That was Rilke. The other wedding vow
we took from *The Little Prince*. A smart fox
tells the charmed boy, "You are responsible

now for your rose." "'I am responsible
for my rose,' the little prince repeated,
so that he would be sure to remember."

Our first year together in Ireland,
a winter of rain-damp in Hollymount,
the bitter house unable to care less

for your narrow moods. One night, at the end
of your rope, we needed to change things up
to palliate the claustrophobia.

You couldn't believe how dismal it seemed,
how suffocating the bare arrangement,
so I pitched an impromptu silliness,

and we crawled over to the bedroom wall,
elbowed our bottoms up, heels over head,
cantilevering deadpan for ten minutes.

Time was quick to quibble, but I see us
propped up still, jarred plumb in upending ways,
bursting open with incredulous mirth.

I regretted our shared fertility.
Our first-born born (nicknamed "The Pinto Bean,"
the size he was, quipped a pre-natal book,

at six weeks' gestation), it was brought home
that sex was to make babies, calendars
marking your cycle of necessity.

The first month that we tried for a second,
bang! A sperm and egg were married for life,
and, called daughter now, have stayed together.

Never happier! Telling, though, how we first
mistook the news we'd hoped for. The pee-strip
showed a clear negative. Discarding it,

we turned in for the night. The next morning,
I don't know why, I took it from the trash,
glimpsed joyful hints of a dividing line.

Tricky when bedmate metamorphosis
leaves the essential bed manners to morph,
and unsteadies them in their own bunkers.

If this was uncommon, we pretended
otherwise. Avowed bonds are surely bound
to be sacrosanct. We had much to prove.

But there were sensitivities we learned
not to trigger, rules for cautious feeling
brought into the house, into the bedroom,

like snipped-off forget-me-nots, forgotten
each time just long enough to let wither,
as new ones would be found and rearranged.

We'd skirt the bed with the familiar blues.
If we found we couldn't breathe, neither blamed
such darling accessories for the home.

Never time to throw in the soiled towel.
Had we tried everything? Clearly not,
but every fix seemed fixy, counterfeit,

and brought us back to who we were, ourselves,
two dumb fucks. Character is destiny,
always reaping what it sows, at both ends

of the parched field. Water it with … my dear,
we *never* use that old wet metaphor.
Filly and stallion, we hoped invention,

not mere necessity, was mare. Our job,
our one simple job, was to stay married,
in spite of all. Was that not proof of love,

love of a certain sort? Be family
to the small souls fetched by our rattled bed,
and practise, like doctors, to do no harm.

We read everything we could get our hands on,
except each other. Books about marriage,
the common varieties and the weight

they put on women, their cultivation,
or what comes to the same thing, their harvest.
Books about how to wake up your marriage.

Communicate! Add bling to the bedroom!
Safeguard yourselves from falling in a rut!
Reinvent the old meanings of nuptial!

Books about how the sole end of marriage
marries all our illusions about love
and then divorces them separately.

Then a book on so-called open marriage,
hidden in plain view among the others,
outlier, single volume, unopened.

We laugh that it was after seven years,
though each of us insisted nothing itched,
that therefore, nothing itching, we were safe

to scratch where we liked, every body part!
In the midst of having our loved "Littles,"
we added a brainchild, an afterthought,

that jealousy is for possessive types,
and solitude an aphrodisiac –
leaving ourselves out – for stolen pleasures.

Our not having sex made us curious
about having sex … not with anyone,
but, not having it, what having sex was,

something that might be detoured otherwise.
How could I know our "marriage of true minds"
set scare quotes around the silent body.

"I wish you joy of the worm," a dear friend,
Linda Munk, once wily said, listening,
knowing I would pick up what she put down.

The portent is whispered to Cleopatra
by her helpless jester, ordered to bring
means to off herself (or get herself off),

an asp curled in a basket. Could I wish
the like for you, my tongue in Shakespeare's cheek?
Open marriages are impossible,

she said, to contain by definition.
Every plus-one's a Pandora's basket.
What you want a hand getting something out of

itself gets out of hand. More than you think's
what you feel. But I wished you joy of it.
Meaning the basket, of course, not the asp.

The love-making *chez nous*, as unforetold,
foretold its course, becalmed in the still air,
and somehow ran aground there, hullside up.

In *The Art of Love*, Ovid volunteers
a cheeky formula: love someone else
and grow tired of neither. On one hand,

it suited our *both/and* clusivities,
but on the other, had little to do
with this faux-celibate predicament.

Not another love, but love's different kinds,
was the muddled grammar we parsed. Love is
what it touches? Love is how you make it?

We winced at the risky puns and jockeyed
to explain telling sentiments apart,
the way it can distinguish want from want.

Your first night with your first. Late afternoon,
imagining I would imagine it
a bond offering, you asked me to help

pick out a suggestive bra from the drawer.
Maybe red, I said, pointing to the blues.
In my head, I was falling in battle,

armies of good intention at the charge –
General Brock's "Onward, York volunteers!" –
screwing dazed courage to the sticky point.

The hour come round at last when lovers
dim their lights, we sat beside each other
on the bed, our daughter Cory and I.

Not yet two, she would never have seen strange
in a grown man beside himself with grief,
letting it all go, as she played with dolls.

We were careful to get the wording right.
This was nothing like infidelity.
In good faith there was mutual support,

encouragement, wanting for each other
all that could be wished, joy for a loved one
enjoying a quick fix. Our constancy

was knotty and more entangling, but still
preferable to the tormented
and possessive guiles whole neighborhoods

mobilized. We had a small ritual
with the kids. Nights one of us was away,
we lit a single candle in the front window,

to help illuminate, they imagined,
the long road home. Reflection in the eyes,
faith was what we burned for, and burning kept.

Unprepossessing, I was glad for you
and the ripped hottie luck dropped beside you
on a WestJet flight home from Calgary.

Flirts flying between, you laughed later
to confess the two of you were on fire
before "No Smoking" went off at the gate!

You played flight attendant, subtly summoned,
and he knew just how to push your buttons,
there as elsewhere, you later gushed and gushed.

Something about how he could grease the wheels
helped things to go more smoothly, you rejoiced,
and I with you. My first urgent answer?

To go off and write more poems, just like me,
about jealousy, the scourge of ego.
My most seductive, if I don't say so.

One time, you left behind a written card,
as you were going out for a hot night.
"Remember, you are the love of my life."

Something for me to gobble up quickly
if the need arose, as I guess it did,
from time to time, back in the lonely days.

I wonder though, was that the right approach,
or one that we believed in even then,
something to say when something to be said

was called for? Our *both/and* intuitions,
handing out equalities all around,
leave scant room for pledges of *either/or*.

You are the only this, the one true that.
Nice ways to think. But we have to play fair,
and leave cards for everyone when we go.

I was slow on the uptake, several years
honing my bumptious and incompetent,
trader in every spectrum innocence.

But rather jolly too, those looking years,
keeping my head up, Fridays at the pub,
mistaking impossible for perhaps.

It took me forever to figure out
what a world of women would never see
in a married guy pretending to keep

his options open. An operator,
user, fast-talking cruiser, narcissist,
out to get anything and everything.

I couldn't understand why everyone
was clucking, when in my stiff autist mode
I walked like a duck and talked like a duck.

One particular line has stayed with me.
Someone I had dated for several weeks
was off to Korea to teach English.

I sat beside her in the airport pub,
killed time and talked about the end of things.
She wanted to explain what hadn't worked

between us. "Too many hours," she said.
"Too many hours?" I questioned, confused.
"No, too many *ours*," she mouthed patiently,

punching the pronoun. First person plural
in the genitive, the fussy tickler
of what belongs to whom, when there is more

than one, and still worse, more than one two:
possessives never singularly whole,
even after you've been taught the language.

But what about the children? people asked.
Will they not lose part of their innocence?
When we opened, they were four and two.

Family became whoever was around.
Plus-ones were simply extras at Scrabble.
In time, if they liked, babysitters, pals,

easy pushovers for ice cream and treats.
There were moments. Cory asked you once
if you loved your boyfriend. You said of course.

But I want you to love Papa! I *do*
love Papa, you said, with a soothing look.
She had to walk, as Henry James would say,

all the way around that one, take it in.
Stevens says truth comes in the simplest word,
almost as part of innocence, almost.

The house routine looked more like nostalgia
for sixties customs, two parents juggling
more grind than they can manage, moonlighting.

Except for us it was magic mirrors.
Kids at home, which of us poked dirty bums
and tossed bedsheets, while the other played?

Lovers would be seconded, babysat
if we were teaching. Choreography!
The house-hive hummed. It was busy being.

Homebodies, we were as far from commune
as one could imagine. Boundaries clear,
nothing was shared that really shouldn't be.

I think of those candles in clay holders
called the circle of friends, each single one
cherishing a flame in warm company.

There's that yarn about how Carl Jung
would have his mistress for Sunday dinners,
joining the couple to triangulate

a square oak table, while the lamb was served.
Our house was open to your carpenter,
who had beautiful hands I always thought.

We even shingled the roof together,
me the Gofer, he the one with an eye
for the snap line, what overlaps with what.

That one year, flirts flitting, you rang my belle,
and she briefly became our mutual friend
à la nothing out of Charles Dickens.

How generous we were, how civilized.
And heartless, not to wince at Carl Jung
asking a wounded love to pass the salt.

Raised a Christian by austere Reformers,
you were taught to be honest and open.
Reap what you sow, it says in the good book.

Then a jilted beau threw the book at you
in anger, and noised it out to your dean
at the religious college that hired you.

The zealous dean came down from the mountain
campus, to get your story whole, he said,
not judge. We both had the awkward feeling

he requested too many juicy facts.
Forthright, you composed yourself, had nothing
to hide. Of course there could be no question

of your staying on, you were told at last,
at a Bible school. Why then, we wondered,
the deep probe? He was reaping what you sowed.

Mental health, doubtless, is a saving grace
when you have it. Clinical depression,
Touretter's tics, the spectrum's what-have-you

not getting it: they keep you on your toes.
Another saving grace, when being there
is not helping, is being where you are.

To be present for each other, we vowed,
if not only for each other, if not
all the time. How to be responsible

for your rose, you little prince, and a prince
to someone else. Well, Saint-Exupéry
would say, for starters, be an alien;

picture impossible things; ask questions,
answer none; do a disappearing act;
and grieve for your sad rose so far away.

O Rose thou art sick, said the English bard.
I guess he'd know, like you an alchemist
of the spirit, like you mad composer

of lone mythologies, fabled, self-made.
Except the worm that would fly in and out
at night kept appearing invisible.

I watched him, frisky, finding out your bed,
look to eat through your independent lives
with his dark unsecret love, succeeding

only with the one. Every storm will howl,
you have learned, make all it touches shattered.
A rose takes a licking in the bad ones.

But watch it as the clouds start opening,
utterly soaked, petals hanging in there,
outlast the worm of any given bloke.

Puzzled by the hard terms, I look them up,
find what they're hiding from me, as though words
might have a little something going on,

two-timing it with four other subjects.
"Jealous" is serviced by an ancient Greek
dependent, goes by the name of *zelos*,

if what I read is true. Word is, this one
has it in for *zeal*, but also, get this,
eager rival; if that's not low enough,

keen imitation has been coming up.
What do you suppose is going on there?
And why am I always the first to know?

Too loose! *Zelos* should have been a sweet thing,
eager, keen, full of zeal. Had the whole world
going for it. I don't get it. What a shame.

I find half the puzzle of relation
made whole in the Greek word *metanoia*,
an after-think, a careful musing-more.

In the Christian book it means repentance,
naturally, if you give it further thought.
You have to carry on, says metaphor,

if you hope to reach open at the end.
Meta of course is meta, in the way
over and beyond are after-effects.

But *noos* is mind and spirit, consciousness
itself, the heart and soul of perception.
Relation then's about how far you think

to take it. Out you go then, have an eye
for the limit, and try to know yourself
at every turn you are bound to repent.

People think of a rock and a hard place,
trying to sort out what they hold on to.
On one hand, the flailings of jealousy.

A love inside you is forcing your nose
to the front glass of a candy store,
while your sugar kisses tempting *bonbons*.

On the other hand, you quit possessing
grabby outrage, but feel the give-a-shit
bleed out of you, as from an open vein.

You're done, finished, empty as all get out.
Either you care what that altered ego
does with her body, or hearing at all

about it is offensive, TMI.
Involvement does most things by halves, holds us
to gimme teasers we shy from owning.

The view that what you give to someone else
you subtract from me, and the opposite.
That is, in every jealous sense, the rub.

There's just so much of oneself to spread round.
AWOLS tallied, you're passing off fake goods
to make up difference, borrowing Paul

to play Peter. That's not the way to think,
open replies. You cannot fill a whole
with anything it is not already.

It is not about your own possessions,
what you can get out of people, but what
(silly time to joke?) you put into them.

Feelings are feelings. The last time I checked,
no one has found a way to add them up.
When you are around, you should be present.

The old solution, they should just divorce!
We threatened it enough, in cold remorse,
in anger, and then thought better of it,

better of us. No one can understand –
not other partners, maybe least of all
ourselves – what aimless possibility

is at work within, some hint that a home
is more and less than just an open house
for folks to come and ogle disrepair,

not a relic of reasons it was built.
Divorce, in the first place, is *either/or*,
frozen hearts dividing up the spoils.

The numbers are up. A tough time is what
everyone is having, we included.
If marriage fails, it was brought home to us.

An affair is sometimes better advised,
advises Ovid in the *Art of Love.*
If open could beat infidelity

as the sweet sauce in time's tango, fetching
one lover to the next over aeons,
would not the other shoe (I'm winking)

have fallen? Affairs can preserve the peace
at home, until they can't. When honesty
itself's at peace, the home's already calm.

Affairs are tried and true, says history,
and best finesse contested middle grounds
between the yes and no, where lovers live.

The trouble with honesty, it has no
final answers, leaves you in the cranny
where nothing left unknown meets finding out.

Skeptic naysayers say "He wants it all!"
A couple of kids, steady wife to watch
after things, of course a little something

on the side, to save him from distraction.
I wonder if that's really what they mean,
wanting it all. All the stress, the scatter?

We all pray vexed afterthoughts in bed:
"If this is it, then also something more,
dear God, if you would." Angling for "not this."

Someone settling for less-than-more is like
a dead body making friends with the box.
But that's not the point. Love is the hard stuff.

Measure out your poison and toss it back.
In other moods, I'm less jaunty. Open
is like aging, not for your feint of heart.

Adjective. *Swinging hindrance put aside,*
affording passage through a barrier.
Of a restricted space, where having part

of the enclosing boundary unlatched
may provide access to the interior.
I found myself double-taking at these

definitions of open, left ajar.
I looked for prophecy and prediction
in lexicons, but the mute diviners,

plumbing the ancient wellsprings of omen,
were poker-faced on what was to be done,
stuck to the fact, the effect all around,

of certain actions on their passive parts.
Adjectives modify the nub they touch.
All the rest can go hang in other words.

The assumptions that people tend to make.
A bunch of swingers! Polyamory!
Those key parties went out in the sixties!

One of them must have wandered – and I bet
it was his hand caught in the cookie jar –
and drove the other to this patchwork thing.

They should learn, life's not just about the sex,
and neither is marriage! Indeed it's not.
I regret this much. Given the carefree

projected on us, couldn't we at least
have had it? The truth was more divided.
Two love vibrators with dead batteries.

We both found perfect imperfect partners,
kindreds to give to everything we had
the sum total of what we didn't have.

It smacks of sister wives, polygamy,
my partner says, when each one knows of each.
The stopping in for gossip, cheese and drinks,

brings the higher out in hierarchy,
which somehow, go figure, there always is.
Honesty only gets you everywhere,

which is no place to be. There's double-think,
things not said are said in the roundabout;
the so-to-speak is deafening. Still worse,

when separate things are kept separate,
the middle that you're caught in's too handy,
too up-to-you. Advantage Jeffery!

What in hell is that? You want to keep peace?
Tend to needs? How many balls can you drop!
There's no advantage in all honesty.

It's not the "understanding" (tongue-in-cheek)
that you have at the house. All's agreed to
and agreeable, settled as Sunday.

It's the special pleading that complicates.
There's your partner-in-love, nearer, more real,
more *face à face*: with passion's chemistry,

the easy all-in's inviolable,
each libido finding its perfect mate,
the one you were meant to know, in that world,

from the beginning (a place where all things
that happen still happen for a reason).
A plus-one is always better at math,

will smell a bait-and-switch, not the favour
of one over another, but the deeps
of mystery bonds, yawning, out of reach.

How to navigate the traps of marriage,
not turn them into other kinds of traps,
and thereby keep it guessing, keep it fresh?

You have to sabotage your own interests
in the interests of an interest greater,
find that greater interesting in itself.

Undermine your own ego, if you can,
lead it by the no's and play tricks on it,
tricks like catch-as-catch-won't, hide-and-don't-seek.

None of this will work of course. Nothing does.
But getting out of metaphoric Dodge,
you become "Experiment in Progress,"

if you get the double gist. Still trying?
Or still making headway? The trap is sprung
with no one in it! You, least of all.

Open marriage, if you ask, is nonsense.
Kant's imperative, categorical,
says never choose an action in the world

you could not recommend to everyone.
Your behaviour must prove a general law,
or you fool yourself, and the rest to boot.

That's a nub. What works for one (or doesn't)
can never guarantee a like result
for the shadow self, looking for answers,

who upsets the apple cart, being you.
Thus, saucy for the goose, out gandering,
makes gander hit the sauce, back in the coop.

There's a more general maxim we possess
that comes in handy here: non-possession,
I own, is nine-tenths of the law in love.

Open marriage is a metaphoric
paradox, as all relations must be,
meaning of course, if you tangle with it,

paradoxically metaphoric
from the start. Your unlikely singles pair
to bring things improbable to life.

Something at the heart of two hopefuls jars
their very being's shared ontology,
their *is and is not*. Says *let it be so*.

Something unbelievable, believed in,
is not so much realized as lived out
according to. It's what bridge engineers

hold out to us. The true lay of the land
is laid aside, so that a made-up way,
thrown out there, becomes possible, far gone.

To hold open. What, as though your partner
were a kind of door for passing through,
unblocking in the manner it gives way?

Which, to think of it, is impossible,
doors being barred holds to begin with,
not the last escape route that a bard holds.

What if open were a state of longing
to cling to, and have, grasping the release,
relinquishing the other's ownsome hold

while accepting it. I remember once
our approaching a set of double doors
so perfectly in stride that we both grabbed

the one nearest and were first to open,
each of us holding the other's gracious
allowance, and blocked by it, so we laughed.

There is of course the unreality,
call it the illusion, of relation,
where you never really live what it is,

never really master the differences,
lifting the *between* by its own bootstraps.
How, when you throw your arms up, ecstasy

and despair are indistinguishable.
As though empathy were on the spectrum.
As though, merely standing where one did,

a mindboggler, a singularity,
open, only with nowhere and nothing
to hide, you had more lives to live than are,

like see-through templates passed each one
over the last, invisible, and on
the life that lies hidden, perfectly clear.

I don't believe that your idealized state,
this way of coexisting you propose,
exists anywhere on earth, or even could,

said Plato's straight man in the *Republic.*
To pull off such a life's impossible
when ideal relations are so iffy.

That may be so, said Plato at his best,
but there is a kind of template for it,
laid up in heaven, which those who wish to

may behold, and beholding, inhabit,
almost as though they lived there, true abode.
We might have asked, had we another chance,

where shall our bodies live in the real world?
But coy Plato, ending the chapter there,
leaves the body to abide wondering.

Plato could use a modest do-over,
a *mise à jour*. The concept that, in love,
we are the broken halves of perfect eggs,

looking to be whole again, as was meant.
A bunch of averages braving the odds!
My serrating edge I hold against you,

looking to find the better half I lost,
and belonged to, long before I was born.
Like democracy, it's a fine idea

if you can crack it. For the rest of us,
it's a recipe to think of oneself
as half an egg. What future is there

imagining all our halves as have-nots?
No one is half of anything. Plato,
am I right? might have sampled scrambled eggs.

Was it about having heart for *both/and*,
not its other, *either/or*? Or better,
the gumption for *both/and* AND *either/or*?

Metaphor always carries me away
toward couplings in a fore-bearing spirit,
tries to believe decisions are for wimps,

and that grace, in relation, is a state
where multiple and singular are one,
if not altogether. I went with it,

and tried to think it through. If my *both/and*
is about more love, not less, how does it
work out for *both/and*'s individuals?

With something of an *either/or* from each,
I serve it back to them, the song and dance
each and either could want, both and neither.

They are shifting centres of gravity,
the fields of love's gravitational fields,
bond's singularity uncentring

what it holds jealously. The pull of vow
and pull of attraction, each with a truish
"I am bound to you" lying through its teeth.

Which says everything by saying nothing
about what it already is, mixed up.
Love's tautological to begin with.

Heartbreak's gimbal pivots on a tripod
that hasn't a single leg to stand on.
There's an uncertainty known to physics,

where the centre among triple masses
can never be found. It is called "the three-
body problem." Some truths speak for themselves.

My study of the atom would suggest
every wedlock is dialectical.
Its dilations collapse, to make a point.

Love and the sex that makes it will divide,
demand security and trust, two rings
circling their wagons against disorder,

against the centre's in-tugged unholdings.
And so it happens. And when it does,
the rounding bonds make bondage, make instress,

and the early somehows that prospered love,
if not dilated into lessenings
(those ghostly hints, let slip, there was a hitch)

must lapse into a schism all the same.
Marriage demands a singular abyss,
certainty falling into the open.

Our moneys are still mixed, life policies
stand still in the other's name, our pensions –
weighing in the balance from *pendere* –

have kept us on a scale, a level true.
One winter, the time and the timing bad,
we tried a separation agreement

witnessed carelessly by stray relatives,
more for anxious partners than ourselves.
Predictably, the idea came unglued.

Too long committed to our status quo
(which gave us little status, and no quo)
I was angling to preserve our promise

as a riddle, an ardour's happenstance,
which, according to misfortune's fortune,
was everyone's to cope with, not just ours.

The thing about us, I suppose, neither
is much good at company. Under sheets
or in a social space, our vectors point

selflessly toward solitude, a place
defined by one's being single in it,
a hunch, each's own ownhood's gravity.

Did I use open to drift? I must have.
The drifting was so long, so gradual,
in my heart I would call it other things.

There was "separation for tax reasons"
(crafty of me, you insisted). House sold,
next was your cottage penthouse, crammed with birds,

my flat in Westdale, snug as a dollhouse,
tight as a bookshelf, drifting and drifting,
a sorry hermit's grotto to cave in.

At something like your metaphoric end
in the sport of love and loss, you exposed
your whole heart to a crafty one, his art

of lying unmastered. I cheer you on,
but you vow now that you're out of the game,
savouring *you* time, not the dating sites,

not doing what men want (which, as a girl,
you *almost* can remember having to).
You fancy telling any guy that asks

to go fuck himself, which may be all
you needed the whole while. But I worry
for your solitude. Not dying alone

(if I'm around, I will make sure you don't),
but where hope for future love expires,
the raised-up hoisted on its own petard.

Your love of horses, how you understood
their place, when, skittish, they seemed to stare
at wheres other than your present else.

How is distance a form of whispering?
An over-there's *I am here*, its say-so
softly said, is too far to be listened.

Ranchers will chase all they like, lassos
or fencing, to rein in the stallion's time
to imagine that all space is endless.

The field must be open, or seem to be
somehow not in a hurry, somehow
looking elsewhere. Let the mustang graze.

With no other side for pastures to be
greener on, it may slowly come to him
that a long time is just what patience needs.

You went from our pent house to a penthouse,
on top of the world, a white cockatiel
yammering on your shoulder to get out.

Weekends, we visit, the children and all:
laughs and catch-up, Uber Eats, while we fight
for the PS 5 remote. With your bong,

my tobacco pipe, we smoke out the long
history, and how, for reasons we trust,
it got us here. Auden's Achilles Shield,

I've said, mocks all ideals. Our give and take
was more literal than we might have wished,
lonelier, more separate, open ended.

But love's a feeling with no single side,
and so is gratitude, and modest pride
at what, our promise kept, the gods have wrought.

I can only parse love's muddled syntax
by claiming independence from all parts,
if you will, of the sentence handed out.

That sets me in parentheses, I wot,
the ego, undecided, self-obsessed,
which outright speakers would close brackets on.

A room of one's own, dear Virginia plugged,
a rabbit hole for the writing rabbit,
and with no one there who is not one self.

Thing to like is, single definitions
can keep clear of simultaneous twains,
attachments that might divide and conquer.

Give me the rent middle, less meddlesome,
the cleft, where a sorted unto-itself
reconciles tugs in the interstice.

Is marriage without sex loveless marriage?
Or is love without sex the deepest love?
Is sex the lonely product of the deep

plash of feeling it drops headlong towards,
the way water will in a waterfall,
to the spume and scum frothing and frothing?

What happens to sex at the rent surface
of deeper love, the quiet pools
never seen clear to the depths of?

Does it burst in upon itself, achieve
its falling aim, pour off its weight, empty,
into some kind of transparent likeness,

or does it vanish, unnecessary
and indistinguishable from the fathom
alone it wanted to but could not be?

The promise (more like premise?) at the start,
that everything happens for a reason.
Were we not half bad at the likely match?

Neither of us had stomach or the skill
for relationships according to Hoyle.
What we were open to, as the nights closed,

was possibility. Not *everything goes*,
not *get your jollies* or *do as you like*,
but giving each benefit of the doubt,

doubts about ourselves, about ownership
and rights, and using them to put more thought,
not less, into the shared autonomy.

If we have grown apart, we've also grown,
apart, in ways that prove – with them's-the-breaks,
with love – we would always have ended here.

We didn't think of a Pandora's box.
A marriage opened up, what could happen?
I would guard your solitude, and you mine,

and the two privacies would saunter off
to lay as they liked, fetching from the roost
the stolen eggs. But somehow after years

of uncompeting existential loves,
ten-year partners joining, not on the side
at all and forming their different centres,

with their own circumference, the centre
we sang on about centring as it moved
marginally centripetal, loosened.

We said it was about more love, not less.
Does love survive more love? Open the box,
my dear, open it. Tell me what you see.

Playing as innocents, we found ourselves
in the belly of the beast, pretending
home was better at sea. Jonah's one sin,

quips the countervailing commentary,
was how, at first, he strove to plug his ears,
keep rote routines cozy and trivial,

gag the pesky inner voice yammering
at him to make trouble for Nineveh.
None of it was courageous. Shall we say

that we were gobbled up and spit back out
by some open-yawning leviathan
whose orphic message was gut wrenching?

I don't mind so much that people turn up
their noses at the whole fishy story.
Only, Nineveh never did thank us.

The question of to be or not to be
open was a crux we hardly troubled.
We wondered instead, is family sacred?

Both raised by parents who rode out marriage,
as Dr Ruth advises, with good sex,
we thought families were to take for granted,

love you don't need to deserve, as Frost says,
for when you go there, they must let you in.
You were just fifteen when your mother died,

left to feel unhoused and undeserving.
If family is foundation, and sacred,
and the sacrosanct a still flexible

hypothesis, a what-if-this-instead,
whatever is misaligned or missing,
you are its open and living welcome.

Thirty years ago you wrote a letter
(licking it closed into an envelope),
wondering how things would be, in marriage,

not knowing if we'd ever open it.
It sticks behind a print of Hamilton,
a faded antique image, where I live.

Did we picture waiting as long as this
to check forgotten prognostications
against the facts of life as we learned them?

Should I unseal those auguries and risk
disappointing who you were? Not just now.
All the joys of regret are in the realm

of possibility (which to this day
is a whole country), and hope is a letter
that leaves past imagined futures unread.

Among the gifts that you have given me,
the unbought ones, the ones that were self-made,
there is one you let go by holding back.

Not held back in the sense of not given,
not deeded continually away
and without expectation of return,

but as an open hand is backward joined
to the heart, releasing the thing it wants
to let be, in a somewhere between.

And the one to whom you give takes it
as a given, whose hold you relinquish,
though it be still yours to give, yours even

when he takes the gift for himself, leaving
what, then, for you to keep giving, for love's
and for his sake, the one you hope he is.

What to call you then, if the itchy time,
the dualling – our double-oh seven? –
is behind us. ("The word is Bond, *Changed* Bond.")

I have someone else too who means the world,
has like rights to the praise in *Song of Songs*
I spoke aloud among the wedding vows.

That makes you friend, mother of our children,
uncontested matriarch, abider,
guard of others' privacy and your own.

Equivocal language of husband, wife,
being variable, leaves Ex dangling
in the equation. Wordplay's duck-and-dodge!

But now I hit a wall, find no double
entendre to wriggle into, or out of,
the words disappearing, my sister, my spouse.

Leaving out our slice of life, some propose
that we remarry, sturdy up those vows
by saying them once more, re-meaning them.

What weakened oaths are we talking about?
That I am responsible for my rose,
that like Rilke we garden solitude?

Thing about renewal, it ages what
it fixes, makes it broken by sequent
definition, the way the rich buy up

houses as tear-downs. We're anything but.
A vow or promise is a kind of place
you learn to move around in over time.

Can a fence walk into an open field
and tell the field it should start again,
and this time at least get on the good side?

A now-dead tree overhears a promise,
a foyer's momentary back and forth:
funny how meaningfulness attaches.

It can make for trouble, not making change
when everything changing still pokes around.
Messy that way, more confusing to all.

People like to be tidier in love,
which I can understand. I've always felt
monogamous by instinct, upbringing,

at least where lovers' passions are concerned.
The one you give your body to, with heart
and soul: those rights are ineluctable.

Which is not to say other hearts and souls
do not have places they might be. Like here.
We don't give everything to anyone.

My plot is at my parents' feet, at White's,
the old ancestral graveyard near Trenton
Air Force Base, where lumbering Hercules

still show sinful souls how to leave this earth,
and head elsewhere, wherever elsewhere is.
Their stone's inscribed "Cooshay and Feddy Doe" –

up the wooden stairs and to sleep – my dad's
last word goodnights, to set my mind at rest.
You're for cremation, I for burial.

Pending who goes first, I'll have to shelve you
(as I had?), until we go dust in arms,
or you'll throw me in the ground, then cut in,

topping the ash hole that you settled for,
to be (and I do hope you're following!)
both together and of the earth a part.

Our gravestone? It's never open and closed!
Some things were clearly carved in slate, *chez nous*.
A lot of other things can never be.

How to write *that* in stone? Entire lives,
undoing divided, spent with others,
who – like even us! – were better suited

to that state of grace, whole hearts and whole minds.
If I have spent my entire body
with another soul, and loved it to death,

as did you yourself, is it becoming
that our bodies lie jointly in this place,
as late espoused, as ardent, like the rest?

I wish you, dear, sweet dreams and a good sleep,
but I imagine we never married
together not together for the rest.

EPILOGUE

A little encouragement, no advice,
from someone who knows sod all about love
but what others taught him he already,

if not alone or altogether, knew.
Honesty is the elixir that comes
last to oneself, which, you'll trust me on this,

is how fibs get told, and how divisions
are seeded where they have no place lying,
the places love can seed. If you let it,

love will mix in all kinds of honesty,
like that family of bindweed that gets around,
rose beds breached, slips for neighbours to sniff at.

But no. Love is the soil not the seed,
ground that will not scatter or multiply,
and always respects its limit, the sky.

THE HUGH MACLENNAN POETRY SERIES

Editors: Allan Hepburn and Carolyn Smart

Waterglass Jeffery Donaldson
All the God-Sized Fruit Shawna Lemay
Chess Pieces David Solway
Giving My Body to Science Rachel Rose
The Asparagus Feast S.P. Zitner
The Thin Smoke of the Heart Tim Bowling
What Really Matters Thomas O'Grady
A Dream of Sulphur Aurian Haller
Credo Carmine Starnino
Her Festival Clothes Mavis Jones
The Afterlife of Trees Brian Bartlett
Before We Had Words S.P. Zitner
Bamboo Church Ricardo Sternberg
Franklin's Passage David Solway
The Ishtar Gate Diana Brebner
Hurt Thyself Andrew Steinmetz
The Silver Palace Restaurant Mark Abley
Wet Apples, White Blood Naomi Guttman
Palilalia Jeffery Donaldson
Mosaic Orpheus Peter Dale Scott
Cast from Bells Suzanne Hancock
Blindfold John Mikhail Asfour
Particles Michael Penny
A Lovely Gutting Robin Durnford
The Little Yellow House Heather Simeney MacLeod
Wavelengths of Your Song Eleonore Schönmaier
But for Now Gordon Johnston
Some Dance Ricardo Sternberg
Outside, Inside Michael Penny
The Winter Count Dilys Leman

Tablature Bruce Whiteman
Trio Sarah Tolmie
hook nancy viva davis halifax
Where We Live John Reibetanz
The Unlit Path Behind the House Margo Wheaton
Small Fires Kelly Norah Drukker
Knots Edward Carson
The Rules of the Kingdom Julie Paul
Dust Blown Side of the Journey Eleonore Schönmaier
slow war Benjamin Hertwig
The Art of Dying Sarah Tolmie
Short Histories of Light Aidan Chafe
On High Neil Surkan
Translating Air Kath MacLean
The Night Chorus Harold Hoefle
Look Here Look Away Look Again Edward Carson
Delivering the News Thomas O'Grady
Grotesque Tenderness Daniel Cowper
Rail Miranda Pearson
Ganymede's Dog John Emil Vincent
The Danger Model Madelaine Caritas Longman
A Different Wolf Deborah-Anne Tunney
rushes from the river disappointment stephanie roberts
A House in Memory David Helwig
Side Effects May Include Strangers Dominik Parisien
Check Sarah Tolmie
The Milk of Amnesia Danielle Janess
Field Guide to the Lost Flower of Crete Eleonore Schönmaier
Unbound Gabrielle McIntire
Ripping down half the trees Evan J
whereabouts Edward Carson
The Tantramar Re-Vision Kevin Irie
Earth Words: Conversing with Three Sages John Reibetanz
Vlarf Jason Camlot

Unbecoming Neil Surkan
Bitter in the Belly John Emil Vincent
unfinishing Brian Henderson
Nuclear Family Jean Van Loon
Full Moon of Afraid and Craving Melanie Power
Rags of Night in Our Mouths Margo Wheaton
watching for life David Zieroth
Orchid Heart Elegies Zoë Landale
The House You Were Born In Tanya Standish McIntyre
The Decline and Fall of the Chatty Empire John Emil Vincent
New Songs for Orpheus John Reibetanz
the swailing Patrick James Errington
movingparts Edward Carson
Murmuration: Marianne's Book John Baglow
Take the Compass Maureen Hynes
act normal nancy viva davis halifax
aboutness Eimear Laffan
twofold Edward Carson
Whiny Baby Julie Paul
Metromorphoses John Reibetanz
Bridestones Miranda Pearson
Dreamcraft Peter Dale Scott
Water Quality Cynthia Woodman Kerkham
Without Beginning or End Jacqueline Bourque
White Lily John Emil Vincent
Kingdom of the Clock: A Novel in Verse Daniel Cowper
SCAR/*CITY* Daniela Elza
At Beckett's Grave Robin Durnford
Empties Neil Surkan
Rush of Wingspan Eleonore Schönmaier
The Electrocutionist Danielle Hubbard
Small Theatres Mark Truscott
Batten Down Su Croll
openbound Jeffery Donaldson